My St

God's People

WRITTEN BY

SARAH FLETCHER

ART BY

DON KUEKER

Publishing House

St. Louis

Unless otherwise stated, all Bible quotations used in this book are from the Revised Standard Version, copyright 1946 and 1952 by the Division of Christian Education of the National Council of the Churches of Christ in the United States of America, or from Today's English Version, copyright by the American Bible Society, 1966.

Concordia Publishing House, St. Louis, Missouri

ISBN 0-570-03426-4

MANUFACTURED IN THE UNITED STATES OF AMERICA

God Makes a World

A long, long time ago God made the world. At first the water and land were all mixed together and covered with darkness. So God made light. Then there was both nighttime and daytime.

Next God put all the water into oceans and rivers and ponds. He put dry land in between. And on the land He put grass and trees and flowers and vegetables. They were very pretty.

God put pretty things in the sky too. He made the sun and the moon and all the shining stars.

Then God decided to make animals. He made fish to live in the water and birds to fly in the sky, and dogs and cats and elephants and zebras and all kinds of animals to live on the land.

"I have done a good job," said God. "But there is one more thing I want to make. A man! He can live in this beautiful world and have fun in it and take care of it."

So God made a man and called him Adam.

God made the world . . .
and it was good.

Genesis 1:1, 31, *para.*

KUEKER

Adam and Eve

At first Adam had fun in the beautiful world God made. He ran through the grass. He smelled the flowers. God even let him name all the animals.

But then something happened. Adam got lonely. He didn't have any people friends.

"This will never do," said God. "I must make a friend for Adam."

So God made a woman and put her by Adam to be his friend. Adam was very happy. He decided to call the woman Eve.

Everything was fine until one day Adam and Eve did a bad thing. They ate some fruit God said they shouldn't eat. Then they got scared. They thought God wouldn't love them anymore.

But Adam and Eve were wrong. God still loved them—very much. He made a promise that someday He would send a very special Person to earth. And because of that Person nobody would ever have to worry again that God would stop loving him.

Do you know who that very special Person is? That's right! Jesus!

God loved the world
and sent His Son.

John 3:16, *para.*

Noah

A long time after God made the world all the people who lived in it became very bad. All of them except one family—Noah and his family.

"Noah," said God, "I am going to send a lot of rain. I am going to cover the whole world with water. But I don't want you and your family to get hurt. I want you to build a big boat and all get inside it. And I want you to take two of each kind of animal with you so they won't get hurt either."

"All right," said Noah, and he did what God said. The bad people laughed at him, but Noah didn't care. And a little later he was very glad he'd obeyed God, because it rained and rained and rained, and all the bad people drowned. But not Noah or his family or all the animals. They were safe in Noah's big boat.

Finally God made all the water go away. Noah and his family and all the animals came out of the boat and said a special thank-you to God for keeping them alive.

"I promise that I will never send all that rain again," said God. "I will put a beautiful rainbow in the sky to remind you of My promise." And He did.

God said,
"The rainbow is a sign of My promise."

Genesis 9:17, *para.*

KUEKER

The Silly People

Once there lived some people who thought they were very strong and very smart. They thought they were even stronger and smarter than God.

"Let's build a tower," they said. "A tower that reaches all the way up to heaven. *That* will show everyone how strong and smart we are."

So they built and built for the longest time, but their tower never got anywhere near heaven.

Finally God said, "I'm going to stop those silly people. I'll mix up the way they talk. Then they won't be able to understand each other, and they'll have to stop building that silly tower."

So that's what God did.

"Hand me another brick, please," said one man to his helper. But what it *sounded* like he said was, "Gibble gooble gurk."

"What did you say?" asked his helper. But what it *sounded* like he asked was "Flivver flavver flee?"

Well, nobody could understand anybody else anymore and so, sure enough, they stopped building their tower. After a while even the part they had built fell down. And everyone knew what silly people they were.

Do your work for God
and all will be well.

Proverbs 16:3, *para.*

Jacob

A man called Isaac had two sons, called Jacob and Esau. One day Jacob pulled a trick on his father and his brother Esau, a really *bad* trick. Esau got angry.

"I'm going to get that Jacob!" he said.

Jacob was afraid of his brother, so he ran away from home. But Jacob was afraid of someone else too—God. He thought God wouldn't love him anymore after he'd been so bad.

One night Jacob had a dream. A wonderful dream. In his dream he saw a beautiful ladder reaching all the way to heaven. Angels were going up and down the ladder, and at the very top was God Himself.

"I still love you, Jacob," said God in the dream. "I will take care of you wherever you go."

When Jacob woke up he felt a lot better. Later he went back home and his brother hugged him.

I will take care of you
wherever you go.

Genesis 28:15, *para.*

KUEKER

Joseph

Jacob had a little boy called Joseph whom he loved very much. Jacob loved Joseph so much that he gave him a special coat, a beautiful coat that was all the colors of the rainbow.

"Thank you, Father!" said Joseph. He was happy. But he had 11 brothers, and they weren't happy at all.

"Why should Joseph get all the good stuff?" they grumbled. And one day they pushed him into a hole and then sold him to some people from the faraway land of Egypt.

These people took Joseph all the way to their country and made him work as a slave. Joseph felt sad, but he never forgot God and he prayed that God would help him.

God heard Joseph's prayers. He helped Joseph make friends with the king of Egypt. Soon Joseph became the king's special helper.

Then one day Joseph's brothers didn't have any more food. They traveled all the way to Egypt and asked Joseph to help them. Joseph remembered how mean his brothers had been to him. But he also remembered how God had taken care of him.

"I want to be kind and love people, like God does," thought Joseph. So he helped his brothers and everybody was happy.

See how much God has loved us!

1 John 3:1, *para.*

The Baby in a Basket

Once there lived a little girl called Miriam, and she had a baby brother called Moses. Miriam was worried because a bad king wanted to hurt her little brother. He sent his soldiers to find the baby.

"We must hide little Moses in a secret place," said Miriam's mother. "I will make a basket for him, and then we'll put the basket in the river. You can hide in the weeds by the side of the water, Miriam, and make sure Moses is all right."

So that's what they did. Miriam hid in the weeds and watched the basket with her little brother in it rocking in the water. *Splish, splash* went the little river waves. "Google goo!" said baby Moses.

Then Miriam heard grown-up voices. It was a princess and her friends! They saw baby Moses.

"Oh, what a wonderful baby!" said the princess. "I want to take him home with me."

Miriam crawled out of the weeds. "Would you like me to find a special baby-sitter for you, Princess?" she asked.

"All right," said the princess, and Miriam ran off to get her mother.

The princess saw how much Miriam and her mother loved baby Moses.

"Why don't you take the baby home with you?" asked the princess. "You can take care of him for me there."

"All right," said Miriam's mother. Miriam felt good. Now the bad king wouldn't hurt her little brother.

God said, "I will be with you."

Exodus 3:12, *para.*

KUEKER

The Strong Man

Once there lived a man called Samson, who was very strong. God made Samson that way because He wanted Samson to help take care of the people who weren't so strong.

One day a fierce lion tried to get Samson. GRRRRR! WHOMP! Samson killed that lion with his bare hands. Not very many people could do that!

But sometimes Samson did bad things. And one day when he woke up, Samson wasn't strong anymore. He felt sad then.

Some bad people captured Samson and made him work for them. Samson had to do it because he wasn't strong enough to get away. But he was strong enough to pray to God. Everybody is strong enough to do that.

"Please help me, God," prayed Samson. And God heard his prayer and made Samson strong again.

God gives me new strength.

Psalm 23:3, *para.*

KUEKER

Ruth

When Ruth was a little girl, she didn't believe in God. She lived in a country called Moab and she didn't really even know about God. But when Ruth grew up, she married a very nice man who told her all about God. Then Ruth believed in Him and she was happy.

After a while Ruth's husband died. Ruth was sad then, but she decided to go with Naomi, her husband's mother, to the land of Israel. She lived with Naomi in the land of Israel, and together they worked in their house and in the fields.

One day Ruth met another nice man. His name was Boaz. They got married and had children. And their children had children and *their* children had children and on and on until one day many, many years later, a special child was born. That special child was Jesus.

I will show the salvation of God.

Psalm 50:23

KUEKER

Samuel

Once upon a time there was a lady called Hannah who wanted very much to have a little baby. So Hannah prayed to God.

"Please, God," she prayed, "send me a little baby. If You do, I will teach him to work for You."

God heard Hannah's prayer and sent her a baby boy. Hannah called him Samuel. She was so happy now!

Hannah taught Samuel all about God, and when he was old enough she took him to the church. There was a nice man called Eli at the church.

"Eli," said Hannah, "will you help teach Samuel about God? He could stay here with you and work for God right in the church."

Samuel thought that was a good idea. So did Eli. So Samuel moved in with Eli and started working in the church.

Of course, Hannah came to visit him. Every year she brought him a new coat. And Samuel grew up to be an important teacher of God's Word.

God made us
and we belong to Him.

Psalm 100:3, *para.*

KUEKER.

The Singing Shepherd

When David was a little boy he spent many days in the rolling green hills, taking care of his father's sheep. Sometimes David had to be very brave. When a bear came to get one of the little lambs, David had to kill it or chase it away. He always prayed to God to take care of him and God always did.

Most of the time, though, the hills were peaceful and quiet except for the BAAA! BAAA! of the sheep. Then David would pick up his little harp and play and sing beautiful songs to God.

Now one day King Saul heard about David's beautiful songs. King Saul was often unhappy because he forgot about God. Sometimes he couldn't even sleep at night. So he asked David to come and play for him before he went to bed. And when he heard David's beautiful songs, King Saul remembered God and he felt better.

When David grew up he became an important king too. But he still played and sang songs to God. Some of them are in our Bible so we can hear them too.

Sing to the Lord, all the world!

Psalm 96:1

Elijah

After a while, some of the people in Israel began to do bad things. They forgot about God and prayed to dolls and statues. God didn't like that. He loved His people and wanted them to pray to Him.

So God asked a man called Elijah to talk to the people.

"Tell them how much I love them, Elijah," said God. "And don't be afraid. I will take care of you."

Well, the people wouldn't listen to Elijah. They got angry with him and wanted to kill him. So Elijah had to run away, far into the desert. There wasn't any food in the desert. But Elijah didn't worry. He remembered what God said and knew that God would take care of him.

And, sure enough, God did. He sent big birds called ravens to Elijah, and in their claws the birds carried food.

"Thank You, God!" said Elijah.

God gives us food when we need it.

Psalm 145:15, *para.*

KUEKER

The Good Queen

Long ago in the land of Persia there lived a king who wanted to find a wife. So he invited all the young girls in Persia to come to his palace.

"I will choose one of you to be my wife and queen of the land," he said.

Now the king had a good servant, a Jewish man called Mordecai, and Mordecai had a beautiful cousin called Esther.

"I'll bet the king would like my cousin Esther," said Mordecai to himself. "I'm going to bring her to the palace."

He did and, sure enough, the king fell in love with Esther and decided to marry her. Everybody was happy—for a while.

But the king also had a bad servant called Haman, and Haman tricked the king into saying that all the Jewish people in Persia should be killed. The Jewish people were frightened.

"Please help us, God!" they prayed. The good servant, Mordecai, decided to ask Queen Esther to talk to the king.

"Make the king change his mind!" begged Mordecai.

"All right," said Esther. A little later the king and Haman came to have dinner with her and she said to the king, "Why do you want to kill all the Jewish people in Persia? I am Jewish too, and so is your good servant Mordecai."

The king looked angry. "I *don't* want to kill the Jewish people," he said. "Haman was a bad man to trick me into saying that. I will punish him."

Then all the Jewish people were happy and thanked God for sending good Queen Esther to help them.

Happy is the person who trusts in the Lord.

Proverbs 16:20, *para.*

KUEKER

Three Young Men

A bad king captured the people of Israel and took them away to his country to work as slaves. The poor people of Israel had to stay in that country for a long time. They had to work hard, and the bad king made up some awful rules.

One of these rules said that the people of Israel couldn't pray to God anymore. They had to bow down in front of statues called idols. Some of the people of Israel just couldn't do that. They loved God too much to do such an awful thing.

"All right!" said the bad king to three young men who wouldn't bow down to the statues. "I'm going to throw you into a furnace full of fire."

"Our God will take care of us," said the three young men. "Even if we die, He will be with us."

But the three men didn't die. They weren't even hurt. God sent an angel to take care of them.

"How wonderful your God must be!" exclaimed the king to the three men. "From now on I won't let anybody say anything bad about Him."

How mighty are the
wonderful things God does!

Daniel 4:3, *para.*

KUEKER

Daniel and the Lions

Daniel was a man who loved to pray to God. He did it every day. But some bad men, who didn't like Daniel, talked the king into making a rule.

"You can no longer pray to anyone but the king!" said the rule.

"I will pray to God *anyway,*" said Daniel firmly and he did.

So the bad men had Daniel thrown into a big deep pit, full of hungry lions.

GRRR! GRRR! said the lions. But Daniel went right on praying. And do you know what? God didn't let those lions hurt Daniel one bit. He sent an angel to shut the lions' mouths up tight. And Daniel stayed in the pit all night, safe as could be.

In the morning the king himself came to let Daniel out.

"I'm so glad you're still alive, Daniel!" said the king. "Your God must be very strong indeed!"

"Yes," said Daniel.

God takes care of people
and rescues them.

Daniel 6:27, *para.*